THE FIRST BOOK OF THE

Arab World

Feluccas still sail the Nile, carrying many kinds of cargo, such as this neatly stacked load of pottery.

The FIRST BOOK of the

Arab World

by Ruth Warren

Illustrated with photographs

FRANKLIN WATTS, INC.
575 Lexington Avenue • New York 22

Library of Congress Catalog Card Number: 63-7581
© Copyright 1963 by Ruth Warren
Printed in the United States of America
by the Polygraphic Company of America

1   2   3   4   5

Contents

An oasis of palm trees is a welcome spot in the vast dry sands of the Sahara Desert.

The Arab People and Their Lands

WHO ARE the Arab people? Where do they live?

If you asked one of the world's 90 million Arabs just why he considers himself an Arab, he would answer you immediately that he speaks the Arabic language — a language for which every Arab has great affection and admiration.

Then he would tell you of the more than two thousand years of history shared by the Arab people, and of the Arab Empire which carried the torch of learning and scholarship for six hundred years while Europe was shrouded in the darkness of the Middle Ages.

He would tell you of the two predominant religions of Arab worshipers — Islam, the majority religion; Christianity, the minority — both cradled in Arab lands, both acting as unifying forces.

He would mention some of the great names of the Arab world: the physicians Rhazes and Avicenna; the great historical philosopher, ibn-Khaldun; the map maker and geographer, al-Idrisi; the philosophers al-Kindi, al-Farabi, and Averroës; and scores of other scientists, astronomers, mathematicians, musicians, translators, and physicians who made a lasting contribution to world science and scholarship.

He would recall some of the outstanding Arab monuments: the Alhambra, the Giralda Tower, and the Mosque of Cordova in Spain; the Dome of the Rock Mosque in Jerusalem; the Umayyad Mosque in Damascus; the Ahmed ibn-Tulun and Sultan Hassan mosques and the Citadel in Cairo.

He would remind you of the Arab wood carving, ceramics, inlaid metalwork, weaving, glass, illuminated manuscripts, tiles, and ivory caskets, which are now housed as priceless treasures in leading museums of the world.

It is this heritage of knowledge, history, language, and religion

1

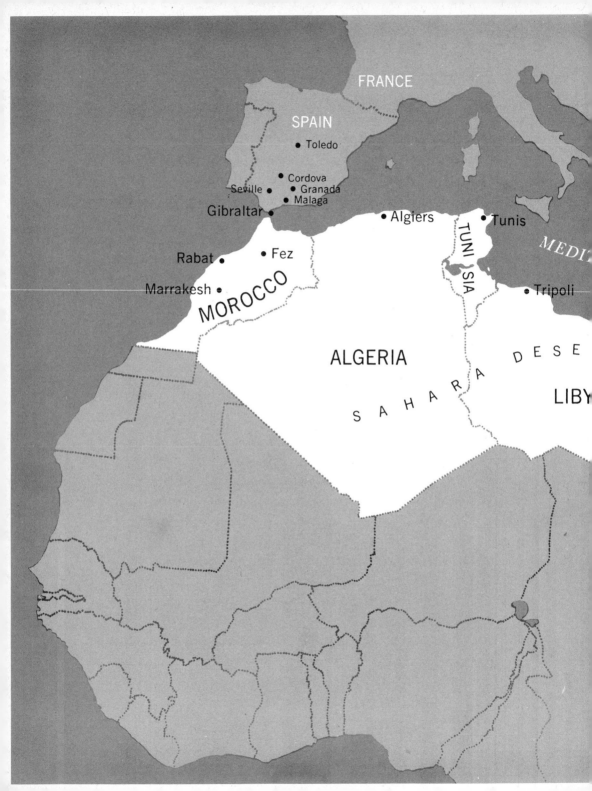

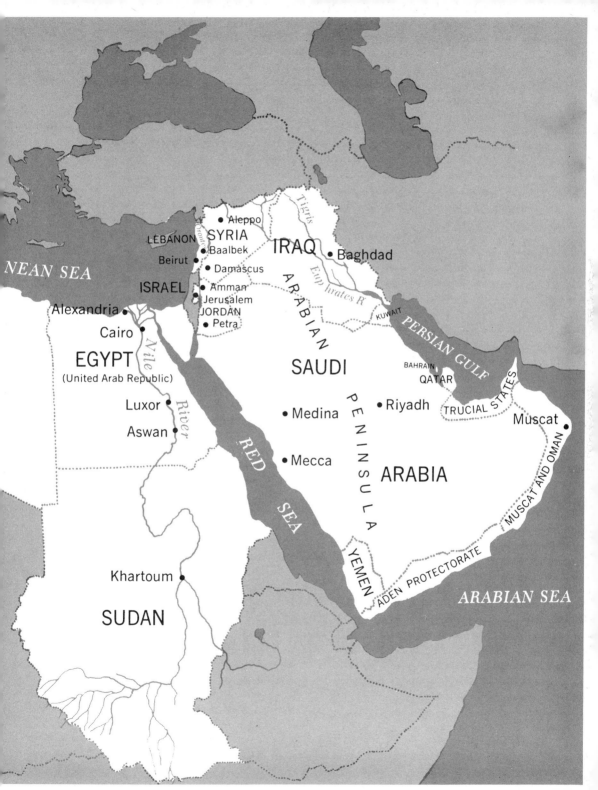

The Court of the Myrtles in the Alhambra, in Granada, Spain, shows the fine decorative work for which the Arabs are noted.

that makes an Arab feel truly an Arab and proud to be one, wherever he may live in the Arab countries.

These are importantly located lands — gateway lands. Algeria, Egypt (United Arab Republic), Libya, Morocco, the Sudan, and Tunisia lead into the continent of Africa. All of these countries except the Sudan border the Mediterranean. Iraq, Jordan, Lebanon, Saudi Arabia, Syria, and Yemen are gateways to the continent of Asia. On the fringes of the Arabian Peninsula are the smaller Arab states and sheikhdoms: Kuwait, Bahrain, Qatar, the Trucial States, Muscat and Oman, and the Aden Protectorate.

Bab Mansour, one of the seventeenth-century gates of Meknes, in Morocco, was decorated with intricately designed green tiles by the Arabs.

Arab lands have few rivers, and no lakes of any importance. The most famous river is the Nile — the longest in the world — which flows for 4,145 miles through the Sudan and Egypt, and empties into the Mediterranean. The twin Tigris and Euphrates rivers, which enclose the area known in ancient days as Mesopotamia, flow through Syria and Iraq to the Persian Gulf.

The search for water is an endless one in Arab lands, for none of these countries has enough water or enough rainfall to meet its needs. All of them except Lebanon have dry and arid deserts of varying sizes, including two of the world's largest: the Sahara Desert and the Arabian Desert.

The climate of all Arab lands is hot in summer, though sea breezes modify the heat of those coastal countries which fringe the Mediterranean; and the mountains of Lebanon, of Syria, of northern Iraq, and of Morocco are cool. Snow caps some of the highest mountains in winter, though this is for the most part a rainy, rather than a snowy, season.

The Arab lands of Egypt, Iraq, Jordan, Lebanon, and Syria are often described as the "cradle of our civilization." In these countries five thousand years ago (and perhaps even earlier) primitive man invented the wheel and the plow. Here the world's first schools were established and the first books were written. The alphabet came from these lands, as did the world's first codes of laws.

Daily Life in the Arab World

THOUGH THE CUSTOMS and habits of the Arab people vary somewhat from country to country, daily life generally follows a similar pattern. The day starts early, particularly during the long, rainless summer which begins in May and continues into November. At sunrise even city dwellers begin to stir, roused from their night's sleep by an unfailing alarm clock, the shouting street vendors. Each vendor has his own call, a description, sometimes poetic and always frankly praising, of his wares or services, whether he is selling eggs, watermelons, fresh vegetables, fish, or a shoeshine.

Most city dwellers live in apartment houses five, six, or more stories high. Every apartment has a balcony or a garden courtyard because Arab people enjoy outdoor living. Wealthy city people either occupy spacious luxury apartments or they own garden-surrounded villas. Professional people and office workers sometimes

A soft-drink vendor roams city streets, ready to serve a thirsty customer.

This woman broadcaster conducts her program with the city of Damascus, Syria, as her background.

live in the suburbs or a nearby village, and commute to work by bus, by train, or by jitney-taxi. Houses in Arab lands are always made of mud brick (adobe), concrete, or stone because there are few forests, and little timber is available.

Men who work daily in offices, banks, and shops wear Western clothes such as a European or an American businessman might wear. In addition to their native Arabic, these city dwellers may also speak either English or French.

Women of the family supervise the household and the children, and do the cooking if there are no servants. Some Arab women have entered professions and have become working wives. There are women doctors, lawyers, judges, interior decorators, journalists, public relations directors, biochemists, teachers, and radio broadcasters in Arab lands today.

Even women who do not go to business often volunteer their services for such charitable activities as the Red Crescent (the Red Cross of the Arab world), the Young Women's Christian Association, the Girl Scouts, the Girl Guides, or organizations working in behalf of orphans, underprivileged children, and the sick.

Whatever the business, social, or charitable duties of the mother or father, the entire family always meets for the noon meal, which is the largest of the day. Offices close for a long lunch hour and do not reopen until three or sometimes four o'clock. The noon meal is a relaxing family meal; no one has to hurry back to work. After lunch there is usually time for a quick siesta in coolly shuttered rooms which keep out the heat of the noonday sun.

For those who seek evening entertainment there are movies

Folk dancers perform against a background of the sixty-foot-high columns of the Temple of Jupiter at Baalbek, in Lebanon.

These men in the customary dress of their native village ride to work on donkey back.

(called cinemas), cabarets, night clubs, and sidewalk cafés. Families often spend one moonlit summer evening a week in a tree-shaded café, drinking coffee and talking with friends. In many cities during the winter season there are concerts, opera, ballet, drama, and folk dance groups. *Son et Lumiére*, the recitation of the past history of famous monuments as powerful lights play over the ruins, is becoming a popular entertainment, and Lebanon's summer festival of music and drama at Baalbek has had many successful seasons.

But the majority of the Arab people live in villages. It is the villagers (and sometimes the laborers and artisans in the cities) who wear the colorful robes which we have learned to associate with Arab lands. The typical dress of a village man is a long robe of cotton (or wool in winter) which slips over his head and reaches to his ankles. It can be any color, according to the fashion of the country or the taste of the wearer. Called a *thaub*, a *gallibiyea*, or a *djellaba*, depending on the land where it is worn, it is a comfortable garment for hot climates. Men may wear one of several types of headdress: sometimes a turban, sometimes a flowing *kaffiyeh* held by a black cord, sometimes a maroon pillbox of felt, sometimes a red felt *tarboosh* (we call it a fez).

In most Arab countries, village women wear flowing black or white robes which reach to their ankles. Sometimes the robe is held in at the waist by a sash, which serves as a satchel for carrying small possessions. Usually a veil is worn over the head and falling to the shoulders. Village women love jewelry — ordinarily, silver bracelets, necklaces, and earrings — and a woman's jewelry is often her bank account. Women are happy if they can afford even one real gold bangle.

HARRINGTON — THREE LIONS

An Arab woman displays typical Bedouin silver jewelry.

Arab boys wear clothes similar to their fathers'.

Village boys wear robes similar to their fathers', and little girls wear straight-cut dresses of printed cotton.

There are, of course, variations in the basic village dress both for men and for women. Sometimes men wear baggy trousers belted at the waist, with a matching shirt. Bethlehem women have a particularly lovely costume — a long black robe cross-stitched with red designs, a wide, multicolored sash around the waist, and a red pillbox hat ornamented in front with rows of coins and covered on top by a long white veil which hangs below the waist.

The veil for women dates back to antiquity, long before the days of Islam or Christianity. It is mentioned both in the Old Testament of the Bible and in the Koran. Though veiling is no longer considered "fashionable" in most Arab countries, women of some Arab cities do veil. Veiling means wearing across the face, up to eye level, a strip of cloth (black or white), which is attached to the woman's head covering.

Villagers are, for the most part, farmers. They are as poor as farmers are over much of the world, and as hardworking. Arab farmers rise early and go to the fields, where they labor all day until sunset. Their wives or children bring them a noonday lunch. A family supper is eaten at home after the day's work is done. It usually consists of bread, beans or semolina, vegetables, and occasionally rice, dates, or other fruit. Meat is a luxury.

Women sometimes help their husbands in the fields in addition to doing the cooking, sewing, mending, washing, and carrying the produce to market. Boys and girls herd the sheep, goats, or water buffaloes, and help in the fields. At night everyone goes to bed early in order to be up at dawn for another long day of hard work.

ARAB INFORMATION CENTER

A young girl wearing a traditional dress of southern Syria plays an ancient instrument called a rababa.

Ever since the days of Archimedes (287-212 B.C.), farmers have pumped water into Egypt's irrigation ditches by using the so-called "Archimedes' screw," as these men do today.

The average farmer's house is of mud brick (adobe) and has little, if any, furniture. The farmer and his family sit on the floor on rugs or matting to eat their meals or to entertain guests. They sleep on the floor or on mattresses which are rolled up during the day. Cooking is done on a primus stove or over a crude fireplace indoors or out of doors. Some farmers are prosperous enough to have comfortable, adequately furnished houses of several rooms, and can afford a few of the luxuries of life.

The larger villages have open-air coffee shops or tea shops where men go to drink Arabic coffee or mint tea, to talk, or to play trictrac, a form of backgammon. Sometimes the coffee shop has a radio. Village women amuse themselves by calling on each other, drinking coffee or tea, and gossiping. Weddings, holidays, and an occasional festival break the monotony of village life.

The Arabs, both city dwellers and villagers, are very polite people. When two friends meet on the street they shake hands and greet each other warmly. *"As-salaam 'alaykum"* is a greeting used in all parts of the Arab world. It means, "Peace be upon you." The reply is *"Wa-'alaykum as-salaam"* ("And upon you be peace"). After their greeting each man inquires about the other's health, and many flowery compliments are exchanged. The two friends shake hands again upon parting.

The Arab people have strong ties of loyalty and a strong sense of responsibility within their family group. They consider it their duty to give help to a member of their family in need, even though he may be a distant relative. Older members of the family such as

Village musicians play for festivals, weddings, and feasts.

grandparents or great-grandparents are cared for as a matter of course by the family. The words of older people are looked upon with respect. Somebody is always helping somebody else in an Arab family. Old people do not have to worry about what will happen to them when they can no longer earn a living. They know there will be room for them, small household duties to perform, and affection from members of the family.

The desert dwellers of the Arab world are the Bedouins, wandering tribes of nomads who graze their camels, sheep, and goats from oasis to oasis in search of seasonal pasturage. The Bedouins live in tents in small tribal communities headed by a sheikh. They eat dates and drink milk from their herds, with occasional meals of rice and roast lamb, roast camel, or birds or gazelles hunted in the surrounding deserts. The Bedouins raise beasts of burden and provide wool from their flocks for the settled residents of oasis towns. How many Bedouins there are we do not know. In the great desert of the Arabian Peninsula there may be five million of them, but this is just an estimate. Some Bedouins breed Arabian horses and hunt with falcons.

Wandering Bedouins pitch their tents in the desert.

The Glory of the Arabic Language

WHETHER they live in towns or in capital cities, in the desert or in mountain villages, all Arabs love the sound of Arabic, their native language. It is a rich language which can be used in many different ways, as each individual speaker wishes. Poets, singers, public speakers, or even an entertaining conversationalist, can enthrall an audience anywhere in the Arab world by their original and imaginative use of Arabic.

One of the pastimes of villagers is to compete with each other in poetry contests. One man will compose a line of verse, his neighbor will answer him in a rhyming line, and the rhyming will go on around a circle of participants. Such a contest sometimes continues at intervals for months, always with an eager and appreciative audience.

Whether or not he is educated, an Arab with a feeling for his language can invent endlessly from a root word by adding to the root or changing it slightly. A prefix, a suffix, a dot, a sign, or an accent can add variety and related meanings to a word. As an example of how an Arabic root word can change, let us take the word *hakama*. It means "to rule," "to decide," "to judge," "to order," "to command." By changing to *hakim*, it becomes "ruler," "governor," "judge." *Hukm* means "rule," "government," "reign," "authority," "decision," "judgment," "decree." *Hikma* means "wisdom." *Muhkam* means "exact," "precise." *Hukuma* means "government." *Hakam* means "arbitrator," "umpire"; *mahkama*, "court," "tribunal"; *muhakama*, "a trial," "a hearing." *Ihkam* means "perfection," "accuracy," "exactness."

Because of its very richness and its endless variety, Arabic is one of the most difficult languages in the world to learn. There are as

17

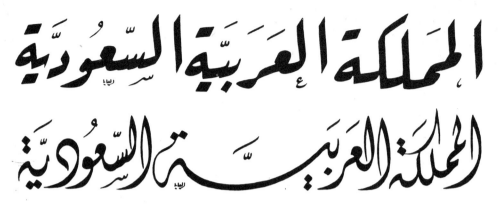

Two types of Arabic writing: the upper, normally used in handwriting; the lower, an ornamental form (from Arabian American Oil Company).

many as one thousand words for "camel" in Arabic, so they say.

Arabic is a Semitic language. Its alphabet has twenty-eight characters, and is derived from Aramaic, the language spoken by Jesus. Arabic looks like shorthand. It is written from right to left.

Arabic can be written so decoratively that for centuries it has been used to ornament wall tiles, mosque lamps, prayer rugs, illuminated manuscripts, and friezes on buildings. There are several styles of decorative Arabic writing. Kufic is one of the most beautiful. Decorative Arabic writing was occasionally used by Renaissance painters in Europe.

Spoken Arabic is quite different from written Arabic. Each Arab country speaks its own conversational Arabic. Sometimes people from Morocco find it difficult to understand people from Iraq, people from the Sudan find it difficult to understand people from Lebanon, and vice versa. But Arabs everywhere can fully understand written Arabic.

The Arabic language has given us many of our own words. Syrup, soda, alcohol, mattress, sofa, admiral, magazine, alcove, cot-

This elegant eighteenth-century emir's palace in Lebanon has filigree carving; marble mosaic; and ornamental Arabic writing on its wall tiles — all decorative arts at which the Arabs are particularly skilled.

19

ton, coffee, sherbet, lemon, cipher, sash, algebra, alchemy, average, arsenal, sugar, and alkali are a few of the numerous words we have received from Arabic.

The first names of boys and girls in Arab lands frequently have a meaning. Among boys' names, Habib means "beloved," Ashraf, "most honored," Nur, "light," Akram, "most generous." Among girls' names are Maha, which means "gazelle," Zein, which means "beautiful," Selwa, which means "to comfort," Dounia, which means "world," Hadiya, which means "gift." Muhammad is the most popular name for boys throughout the Arab world. It means "praised."

The Arab people have always delighted in the sound of their language. Poetry contests were held many hundreds of years ago. Storytellers still entertain spellbound audiences with age-old tales in the bazaars and coffee shops of Arab cities and villages. A favorite tale is "Majnun-Layla," the romantic story of a young man who loved a beautiful girl, Layla, hopelessly. Her father had promised her to another suitor. So for the rest of his life the young man wandered distracted in the desert, singing praises of his beloved one.

A favorite children's book in the Arab lands is *Kalila wa Dimna*, a book of animal fables. Kalila and Dimna are two jackals, and brothers. They are very crafty, and get themselves and others into numerous difficulties. The book also has stories about owls, tortoises, apes, cats, and doves. The French writer La Fontaine is said to have used it as a source book for his famous *Fables*. The story of "Ali Baba and the Forty Thieves," and of "Ala-ed-Din (Aladdin) and His Wonderful Lamp" are favorite children's stories from *The Arabian Nights*, which in Arabic is called *Alf Laylah wa Laylah (The Thousand and One Nights)*.

The Religion of Arab Lands

IN EVERY ARAB CITY every day at sunset you will hear (and perhaps see) *muezzins* calling people to prayer from tiny balconies atop the towering minarets of mosques. It is a peaceful and serene sound to hear the chant, *"Allahu akbar, la ilaha illa Allah"* — "God is great, there is no God but God" — as the day ends and the rose and gold colors of twilight envelop the huge domes and minarets of the mosques.

Five times each day this call to prayer comes from the mosques, which are the "churches" of the Muslims, who represent the religious majority in Arab lands. The Muslims' religion is called Islam, which means "submission to God." Their prophet is Muhammad. They worship God, whose name in Arabic is Allah. Muslims do not like to be called Mohammedans, since their worship is directed

From the balconies of slender minarets, the muezzins *call Muslims to prayer. Al-Azhar Mosque, shown in the picture, houses one of the oldest universities in the world.*

to God, not to Muhammad. The Koran is the Muslim Bible and contains the revelations and teachings of Islam. The holy city of Islam is Mecca in Saudi Arabia. Friday is the Muslim Sabbath.

The Prophet Muhammad, who established the religion of Islam, was born in Mecca in Arabia about A.D. 570. His parents died before he was six years old. At the age of twenty-five, he married a wealthy widow, Khadija, a woman of noble character.

As the years passed, Muhammad retired more and more to a solitary hillside outside Mecca to think and to meditate. There he received visions and revelations of God which sent him teaching and preaching among his people, the Arabs. His wife, Khadija, was one of his first converts. Slowly he gathered disciples, exhorting them to believe in one God, all-powerful Creator of the universe. Muhammad died in 632.

The divine revelations given to Muhammad in visions became the Koran, the Muslim Bible. The scattered fragments of Muhammad's teaching, which form the Koran, were collected by abu-Bakr, first caliph (successor) about a year after the Prophet's death. An official standard text was assembled and approved during the rule of the caliph Othman (644-656) and became not only the Bible of Islam, but has continued down the centuries to be the standard for written Arabic.

Unlike most religious faiths, Islam does not have any ministers or priests. But every Muslim knows the Koran, which is taught him from childhood, and he knows the five obligations of his religion. They are (1) confession of faith — that there is only one God, and Muhammad is the prophet of God, (2) prayer five times a day, (3) almsgiving to the poor, (4) fasting for one month each year (Ramadan), and (5) a pilgrimage to the Holy City of Mecca, if such a journey can be managed. Muslims revere Christ, Moses, and Abraham.

Before entering a mosque a person, instead of removing his shoes, may cover them with canvas slippers.

Before entering a mosque, Muslims and non-Muslims remove their shoes or cover them with canvas slippers. This is an act of reverence. Mosques in large cities are often magnificent, with graceful arcades of columns, lofty domes ornamented with lacelike filigree or stalactites, and stained-glass windows. The floors are often of marble, and the walls are designed of inlaid mosaic in geometric patterns. Sometimes colored tiles with quotations from the Koran in beautiful calligraphy (decorative writing) are used for ornamentation.

A mosque has no seats. People kneel on oriental rugs to pray, facing Mecca. Its direction is indicated in every mosque by a recessed niche called the *mihrab*. There is also a *minbar*, a pulpit, in every mosque; it is approached by a short flight of stairs. The *minbar* is often made of marble or wood, richly decorated with carving or mosaics.

Every Friday a special service is held in mosques. A *khatib* usually speaks from the *minbar*. He is not a minister, but a respected person in the community. The man who leads the congregation in prayer is the *imam*. Both the *khatib* and the *imam* may earn their living at some secular profession. In larger mosques a *sheikh* is responsible for the care of the mosque. The *muezzin* is usually paid to ascend the minaret and call people to prayer. Muslims can pray anywhere; they have no obligation to go to the mosque. It is a community gathering place, a place to rest, to meditate, to read the Koran, as well as a place of prayer.

One month each year, called Ramadan, Muslims are supposed to fast. This means that they do not eat anything or drink anything, not even water, during the hours of daylight. Daylight is considered to start when a white thread can be distinguished from a black thread. Daylight ends when the sun drops below the horizon. A cannon or gun sometimes announces the end of the day's fast. Ramadan corresponds to the Christian Lenten fast, though it is much more exacting. Going all day without even a drop of water in the burning heat of summer requires great devotion and self-denial. The Ramadan fast is meant to give men a closer feeling for God, to give them an opportunity to atone for their sins, to focus their thoughts on what it means to be hungry, and to develop sympathetic appreciation of the plight of those who have no food, or are too poor to buy food. The month of Ramadan varies according to the Muslim lunar calendar, which is different from the Western calendar.

In every mosque a niche called the mihrab *indicates the direction of Mecca, which Muslims face when they pray.*

The mosque's minbar, *or pulpit, is approached by a short flight of steps.*

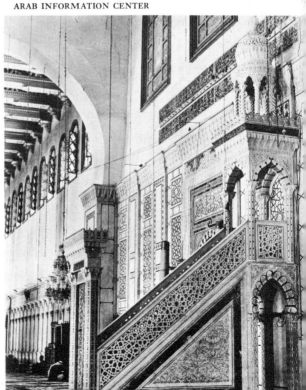

Over one million pilgrims from seventy countries (but chiefly from the Arabian Peninsula) go to Mecca each year to participate in the annual pilgrimage, or *hajj*, which takes place in the twelfth month of the Islamic year. The ritual performed there takes about four days. Each pilgrim wears an *ihram*, two seamless sheets wrapped about the body, symbolically making all men equal in the sight of God and indicating the giving up of worldly things.

The ritual performed at Mecca includes seven circuits of the Kaaba, a huge, cubelike structure of basalt blocks which stands in the center courtyard of the Great Mosque. These circuits must be made on three designated occasions, with prescribed accompanying prayers. They represent man's search for God.

The "Standing before God" is another important ritual. It takes place at 'Arafat, about fifteen miles from Mecca. Pilgrims stand bareheaded until sunset near the Mount of Mercy where Muhammad preached his farewell sermon. Meditations on this occasion are directed to the Day of Resurrection.

The "Stoning" is another symbolical rite. It takes place where Abraham was tempted three times by the devil, and pilgrims stop to cast pebbles at three stone pillars as they wend their way to the Field of Sacrifice to celebrate 'Id al-Adha, the high point of the *hajj*. It commemorates Abraham's willingness to offer his son as a sacrifice to God, who sent an angel with a ram as a substitute. A sheep, a goat, or a camel is sacrificed by each pilgrim, and all or part of this sacrifice is given to the poor. Two final circuits of the Kaaba are made before the pilgrimage ends in Mecca.

The *hajj* to Mecca gives Muslims from all over the world a sense of brotherhood and unity, an occasion to thank God for his compassion and mercy and to express their readiness to submit to his will.

The Islamic religion has several sects, just as the Christian religion

The Kaaba in Mecca, Saudi Arabia, is a venerated place of worship, particularly at the time of the annual Muslim pilgrimage, or hajj.

does. The most important are the Sunnis, who represent the majority of Muslims, and the Shi'as, who are found chiefly in Iraq and Iran. Altogether there are about 430,325,000 Muslims in the world today, and Islam is the second-largest world religion.

Not all Arabs are Muslims. There are many Arab Christians, particularly in Lebanon, where about 50 per cent of the population is Christian. In Jordan, Christian Arabs number about 12 per cent of the population, and there are many Christians in Egypt and Syria. Christian churches are to be found in the major cities of the Arab lands.

Building the Arab Empire

CENTURIES AGO, before the days of Islam or Christianity, the Arabs were known as Arabians. They lived in the arid, almost waterless deserts of the Arabian Peninsula, wandering from oasis to oasis with their herds of camels, sheep, and goats. They belonged to the Semitic family of races. Occasionally waves of Arabians migrated to the more fertile lands of the Tigris-Euphrates Valley, to the Nile Valley, or to the coasts of Palestine.

As early as the first thousand years B.C. there were organized states in southwestern Arabia, the most notable of them being the Minaean, the Sabaean, the Ausan, the Qataban, and the Hadhramaut.

The most outstanding of early Arabian kingdoms was founded by the Nabataeans, who made Petra, now in Jordan, their capital in about 300 B.C. The Nabataeans were extraordinarily able hydraulic engineers and really made the desert blossom like the rose. Many of their cisterns and aqueducts are still in use today. About the time of Christ, the Nabataeans extended their kingdom as far north as Damascus.

For the most part, however, the Arabians wandered in tribes ruled by a sheikh, or chief. These tribes were often hostile to one another, and raided one another's camps, capturing camels and herds. They were pagan in religion, and much afraid of *jinns*, unfriendly evil creatures who, the Arabian tribes believed, lurked in lonely areas of the desert.

It was Islam, preached by Muhammad, that united these wandering Arabian tribes, and not only gave them a religion with one God, but a sense of their own destiny.

The Khaznet, or "Treasury of Pharaoh," is one of the beautiful monuments in the rock-carved city of Petra, in Jordan.

After the death of Muhammad these new converts to Islam became eager to spread their new faith to neighboring lands. Less than a year after the death of the Prophet these desert Arabs of Arabia, a few thousand strong, were on the march, riding northward on camels and horses, to face the armies of the Byzantine and Persian empires. Their foes were superior in numbers, in weapons, and in organization. But the Arabs were not afraid. Their religion gave them a sense of brotherhood, of unity, of purpose. Town after town in Syria fell before them, including Damascus, believed to be the oldest city in the world which has been continually occupied.

By A.D. 646, all of Mesopotamia was conquered and the march went onward through Persia to the Indus River.

Another contingent of Arab troops had by this time moved westward from Arabia toward Egypt. This ancient land of the Pharaohs, including the mighty city of Alexandria, was subdued with little resistance.

The Arabs pushed on through present-day Libya, Tunisia, Algeria, and Morocco, with the Berbers of Africa joining them as converts and recruits. And the end was not yet.

In A.D. 710, four hundred foot soldiers and one hundred horsemen crossed from North Africa into Spain. Encouraged by successful skirmishes, Tariq, a Berber, landed with an army near the Rock of Gibraltar, and vanquished the Visigoth Roderick in 711. Gibraltar has ever since borne the name of this Arab leader (Jabal (Mount)-Tariq in derivation). The Arab armies continued their victorious march into Toledo, Cordova, Malaga, and Seville. Raids were even made into France, but there the Arabs met defeat at the hands of Charles Martel at the Battle of Tours in 732.

In the brief one hundred years since the death of Muhammad, the Arabs had built a vast empire. It reached from the Atlantic

The Rock of Gibraltar is named for an eighth-century Arab leader.

Ocean to the borders of China, from the Aral and Caspian seas to the Arabian Sea. It was larger than the Roman Empire had been at its height.

Historians tell us that the Byzantine and Persian empires were ready for collapse in the Middle East, and that the Arabs only gave them their deathblow. But however you try to explain how and why the Arabs, at first numbering only a few thousand, could build a mighty empire in one hundred years, it still remains an amazing and superlative achievement.

31

Ruling the Arab Empire

A SUCCESSION of caliphs ruled the newly founded Arab Empire. The caliphs (the word means "successor") were considered to be the successors to the Prophet Muhammad, both in worldly and religious matters. During his lifetime Muhammad had acted as head of state, army general, and judge, as well as spiritual leader.

There were three major caliphates. The First Caliphate (632-661) had its capital at Medina, where Muhammad is buried. The Umayyad Caliphate (661-750) ruled from Damascus, where the caliphs surrounded themselves with luxuries from their conquered lands, and attracted poets, scholars, and musicians to their court. During the Abbasid Caliphate (750-1258) the Arab Empire reached its peak and the Golden Age of Arab civilization. Its capital was at Baghdad.

The vast Arab Empire was divided into provinces, over which governors and viceroys ruled. The word "Arab" no longer meant "Arabian," a man of the desert; all conquered people became Arab citizens, whether or not their previous nationality had been Syrian, Berber, Persian, Indian, or Turkoman. Arabic was spoken throughout the empire, and its citizens became Arabized in their culture, their way of life, and their historical traditions.

Damascus, believed to be the world's oldest continuously inhabited city, is bordered by green fruit groves at the desert's edge.

The Crusaders built the mighty Krak des Chevaliers (Castle of the Knights) during their stay in the Holy Land.

33

Many conquered people accepted Islam as their religion. They intermarried with Arabians. Some Christians and Jews preferred to keep their own religion and were allowed to do so. They lived in peace with their new Arab neighbors and were not oppressed. For a short time Christians and Muslims even shared the same church in Damascus — a church that had once been a pagan temple, and later became the Umayyad Mosque.

The Arab Empire, to which this diversity of people belonged, is sometimes called the Islamic Empire, because its origin and culture were Islamic.

During the Abbasid Caliphate the Arab Empire began to break up politically, though its religion (Islam) and its language (Arabic) continued to give it a certain unity. In Spain, a prince from the former Umayyad Caliphate became ruler. In Morocco and Algeria the Idrisids established a dynasty, and in Egypt there was a succession of dynasties — the Tulunids, the Fatimids, the Ayyubids, and the Mamluks.

The founder of the Ayyubid Dynasty was Saladin, whose chivalry during the Crusades (1096-1291) has been widely celebrated in song and story. Saladin never met his famous opponent Richard the Lionhearted, but the two men exchanged presents and communications. During the Crusades, Europeans and Arabs learned to respect each others' way of life. The Crusaders took back to Europe with them such fruits and plants as sesame, millet, rice, lemons, melons, apricots, and scallions. They acquired an appreciation of spices and perfumes, learned to wear satin and damask, and first tasted sugar in Arab lands.

As the Crusades drew to a close, the Arab Empire, after more than six hundred years, was also nearing its end. The preliminary death-blow came from barbaric Mongol hordes, lead by Hulagu, who

The Citadel (at left of photo) at Aleppo, is a famous Arab monument which dates to the days of Saladin.

ARAB INFORMATION CENTER

arrived in 1258 in a whirlwind of raiding and plundering. The Mongols captured Baghdad, burned many of its beautiful palaces, and destroyed priceless manuscripts. Tamerlane and his ruthless Tartars came in 1400, capturing Baghdad, devastating Aleppo for three gruesome days, and carrying away the skilled artisans of Damascus into captivity in Samarkand.

Stunned by these shattering attacks, the already tottering Arab Empire easily fell to the Ottoman Turks, who conquered Syria, Iraq, Egypt, and North Africa in the early sixteenth century. The Ottomans, who were not Arabs, but were Muslims, were to rule Arab lands (with the exception of Morocco) for some four hundred years. The Arab dynasty in Spain had previously fallen to Queen Isabella and King Ferdinand in the year 1492, the same year that Columbus discovered America.

The rule of the Turks cut the Arab world off from the West. This long period of withdrawal while the Western world passed through the industrial age into the atomic age left Arab lands lagging far behind other nations of the world.

The Arab Empire's Legacy to the West

WHEN they left the deserts of Arabia, the Arabs brought with them their language, their religion, their poetry, and an extraordinarily keen intellectual curiosity. As soon as they were exposed to the Greek mathematics, astronomy, medicine, and philosophy in their conquered lands, the Arabs felt a driving urge for more knowledge. It is because of this inquisitiveness that the Arabs were able to leave an important legacy to the Western world.

Syrians, Persians, and Egyptians in the Arab Empire were put to work translating Aristotle, Galen, Hippocrates, Archimedes, Euclid, Ptolemy, and Plato into Arabic. Arab scientists and scholars and philosophers studied these works and wrote commentaries on them during the some six hundred years that the Arab Empire lasted. Arab historians added a new note to history — the sociologic approach, which emphasized the study of human groups and the relationships between them.

During this time Europe was passing through the Middle Ages (sometimes called the Dark Ages). It was the Arabs who preserved precious Greek manuscripts, to be rediscovered by Europeans in the approaching Renaissance. Learning reached Europe during the Middle Ages across an "Arab bridge." Translations and commentaries on such subjects as algebra, geometry, astronomy, medicine, trigonometry, ophthalmology, chemistry, botany, and geography crossed this "Arab bridge" at Spain, at Sicily, and from Syria. Arab commentaries were used as textbooks in the universities of Paris, of Bologna, and of Naples even as late as the seventeenth century.

During the Middle Ages, European students frequently came to study at Arab universities, particularly the University of Cordova. Such European scholars, and patrons of scholars, as Pope Sylvester II,

Dante, Thomas Aquinas, Roger Bacon, and Frederick II of Sicily acknowledged their debt to Arab scholars.

Things, as well as ideas, crossed the "Arab bridge." Paper and the magnetic needle, though invented in China, were passed along to Europe through Spain by the Arabs. The zero and Arabic numerals, though Indian in origin, reached Europe from the Arab world. Numerous textile weaves of Arab origin crossed the "Arab bridge" — baldachino, muslin, fustian, damask, satin, atlas, and tabis.

Metal inlaying, illumination of books and manuscripts, glazed faience pottery, heraldic devices, the arabesque and geometric motives in decorative art, tooling of leather bookbindings, and decorative wall tiles were all passed on to Europe. European architects during the Renaissance adopted many features of Arab architecture: the pointed arch, stalactite ornamentation, and carved inscriptions handled as decoration.

Arab craftworkers are experts at tooling leather.

Cairo's Ahmed ibn Tulun Mosque, with its ramplike minaret, was built by the Arabs in the ninth century.

Many beautiful buildings dating to the Arab Empire are still standing for us to see and admire today. The Alhambra in Granada, Spain, an ethereal fairyland palace, was built in the thirteenth and fourteenth centuries. The Mosque of Cordova, in Spain, now a Christian cathedral, was built in the eighth century. The Hassan Tower at Rabat, Morocco (twelfth century), the Dome of the Rock Mosque in Jerusalem, Jordan (seventh century), the Kairawan Mosque in Tunisia (eighth century), the Ahmed ibn Tulun Mosque in Cairo (ninth century), and the Citadel at Aleppo (Haleb), Syria (twelfth century) are a few of numerous outstanding Arab Empire monuments.

Arab Lands Today

TODAY most of the Arab countries are independent and free. Twelve belong to the United Nations. Eight countries are republics, and four are monarchies. The others are sheikhdoms, on an independent or semi-independent basis. Eight countries have equal suffrage for men and women. Thirteen belong to the Arab League, an organization formed to promote their mutual interests.

Several Arab countries have only recently become free. The reason for the long delay in obtaining freedom is that after the Ottoman occupation ended, European powers moved in on Arab lands. France occupied Algeria in 1830, and established a protectorate over Tunisia in 1881. Italy occupied Libya in 1912. Lebanon and Syria became French mandates after World War I, and Iraq and Palestine became British mandates. British occupation in the Sudan dated to 1898.

Though Arab lands were in contact with the West during the period of occupation and mandates, little social or economic progress was made. Education was available to only a small part of the Arab people, and it did not prepare them for self-government or for the requirements and problems of an industrial and an atomic age. Illiteracy was widespread. Throughout the Arab world there was lack of technical know-how, lack of adequate health facilities, and great poverty. The newly independent Arab countries had literally to start at the bottom of the ladder. They faced the Herculean task of quickly catching up with other countries and of building a new life for their people.

One cloud still loomed on the horizon for the Arab world. For a number of years, Zionists, a Jewish group whose aim was to colonize in Palestine, had been settling in British-occupied Palestine in increasing numbers. When the British mandate in Palestine terminated in 1948 and British troops were withdrawn, fighting broke out. The Palestinian Arabs had no arms, no way of defending themselves. They fled from their homes, and the Zionists took over Arab property in Palestine, declaring a new state of Israel. The whole Arab world was aroused by the fact that one million Arabs had been made homeless and forced to evacuate lands where they had lived for some 1,300 years. The Palestinian refugees sought sanctuary in neighboring Arab states, where they still live in refugee camps. They await the carrying out of the United Nations resolution of 1948, which calls for resettlement of the Palestinian Arab refugees in their homes in Palestine, or for compensation to those who do not wish to go back.

A view of Beirut, in Lebanon, and the Mediterranean Sea.

Earning a Living

EVERYWHERE you go in Arab lands you will see men working in the fields or cultivating date groves, olive groves, or groves of other fruits. The Lebanese and Yemenite farmers will be terracing the slopes of mountains to raise their crops of wheat, barley, millet, fruit, or coffee. In Iraq, farmers will be climbing tall date palms to harvest the dates for which this country is so famous. Syrian farmers will be planting millet, wheat, maize, tobacco, and rice, in the rolling, fertile fields along the Orontes and Euphrates rivers. In Tunisia you will see men working in olive groves which often contain thousands of trees set out in symmetrical rows. Egyptian farmers will probably be harvesting sugarcane or picking cotton. Small boys (and sometimes girls) in all the Arab countries will be tending cattle, flocks of goats, sheep, herds of camels, or water buffaloes.

About 75 per cent of the people who live in Arab lands earn their living by farming. For centuries, farmers have toiled from dawn to dusk to eke out a bare existence. They have used antiquated plows and farm implements. They have winnowed their grain by hand. They have painstakingly terraced the sides of treeless mountains to catch and hold rainwater. They have been plagued by locusts; by drought; by ever-encroaching deserts; by lack of water; by such diseases as bilharziasis, trachoma, tuberculosis, and malaria; and by the demands of the landlords for whom they have worked.

But today things are looking better for the farmers of the Arab lands. The new Arab governments are introducing scientific farming methods and modern farm implements. They are engaged in irrigation projects to make more arable land available. Among such projects are those on the Litani River in Lebanon, the Tigris-Euphrates rivers in Iraq, the Yarmuk-Jordan rivers in Jordan, the Nile River in

41

These farmers still use sieves for winnowing their wheat — a primitive and time-consuming method.

Egypt, and the Blue Nile in the Sudan. Many Arab governments have distributed to the farmers land once owned by large land-holders. Health centers, social centers, better housing, and more schools are in the blueprint stage or are already available in farm areas.

Though industrial plants are to be found in Arab lands, they are mostly for light industry: manufacturing cement, flour, olive oil, cigarettes, footwear, bricks, roofing tiles, soap, matches, clothing, and electric light bulbs, and tanning, food canning, wool processing, and sugar refining. Egypt and Syria have large textile-spinning and -weaving mills, and Egypt has a shipyard at Alexandria, a fertilizer plant at Aswan, and coke plants.

Some of the Arab countries, particularly in North Africa, have rich mineral resources: phosphate, manganese, copper, lead, tin, iron, zinc, coal, mercury, and gold.

Oil is the Arab lands' greatest natural treasure. The largest crude oil reserves in the world are to be found in Arab territory. The sheikhdom of Kuwait on the Persian Gulf leads the list of oil-rich states, followed by Saudi Arabia, Iraq, and Qatar. Libya promises to be another of the important oil-producing countries of the world, and oil has been found in Algeria and Egypt.

At an agricultural training center in Libya, students learn to use mechanical threshing equipment.

A lock-gate in Sudan's Gezira Irrigation Scheme, a cooperative effort between farmers and the government. The main dam is at Sennar, on the Blue Nile, and water is fed to the area through some 3,000 miles of channels.

American companies have concessions in Kuwait, Saudi Arabia, Iraq, Qatar, Trucial States, Muscat and Oman, Aden Protectorate, Bahrain, Tunisia, Egypt, Libya, and Algeria. Thousands of Americans have lived and worked in the oil fields, particularly in Saudi Arabia. Many American chilren have been born in Saudi Arabia, have attended school there, and have learned to speak Arabic fluently. By living and working together, Americans and Arabs have acquired a greater appreciation of each others' abilities, beliefs, and cultures.

To Arab countries, oil has meant that men have learned new skills. It has meant a higher standard of living. It has meant the growth of private enterprises such as trucking concerns, tile factories, and cement factories, which contract with oil companies for their services. It has meant more schools, and better technical training for boys and girls. Even countries without oil often have oil refineries which have contributed to their national economy.

Tourism is another livelihood of Arab lands. Saudi Arabia leads all Arab countries in the number of its annual visitors. More than 900,000 Muslims from the Arabian Peninsula, and more than 200,000 from other parts of the world visit Mecca each year at the time of the Muslim pilgrimage. Egypt also receives a large number of tourists who come to see the Pyramids, the Sphinx, and the monuments of Luxor. Lebanon's cool and scenic mountains attract many summer visitors. Jordan welcomes pilgrims from many lands who come to visit its Biblical sites at Bethlehem, Jerusalem, Jericho, and the Jordan River. Visitors bring needed money into Arab lands, and give work to the people who provide them with hotel accommodations, food, and transportation.

ARABIAN AMERICAN OIL COMPANY

A young Saudi Arabian whose ancestors were wanderers in the desert has become a skilled worker for an oil company.

The Garden of Gethsemane in Jerusalem, Jordan, adjoins the Church of All Nations, with the Russian Orthodox Church of St. Mary Magdalen in the background.

Going to School in Arab Lands

IN EVERY ARAB COUNTRY you will see boys and girls in pinafores, the girls often wearing hair ribbons, going to school carrying satchels of books. These are the lucky children, for there are not enough schools in Arab lands to accommodate all the boys and girls who want to attend them. Some countries have been faced with the dilemma of having from 50 to 180 children in a class. Sometimes pupils go to school in shifts, so that all may have a turn.

The reason many Arab lands lack enough schools is that occupying powers, who ruled Arab countries for so many years, often paid little attention to educating the children of the country, particularly in their native language. And so, newly independent Arab lands have suddenly been called upon to provide a full-fledged school system to meet the needs of their children. It is impossible to create a school system overnight. It takes money to build schools. It takes time to build schools. It takes time, also, to train teachers, to write textbooks, and to translate scientific and technical books into Arabic.

All Arab countries have free public schools *in principle*, even though they cannot yet provide enough schoolrooms and teachers. Most countries have a five-, ten-, or fifteen-year educational goal toward which they are working to make education available to all children, and to make it compulsory. They hope to establish as soon as possible a complete system of primary, elementary, high school, vocational, and teacher-training schools.

Among the really fortunate children of Arab lands are those who live in the oil-rich sheikhdom of Kuwait. These children not only have free education, but are provided as well with free books, stationery, food, transportation, medical services, medicine, and uniforms — from kindergarten through secondary school.

47

المدرسة الثانوية للبنات

Schoolchildren out-side their school in Tunisia.

Eight Arab lands have one or more universities, and in some of the other countries universities are in the blueprint stage.

The two oldest universities in the world are to be found in Arab lands: Al-Azhar in Cairo, Egypt, and Kairouine University in Fez, Morocco. Al-Azhar University dates from 970. The exact founding date of Kairouine as a university is not known, though the mosque in which it is located dates to 861. Both these universities have been religious colleges for centuries, teaching the Koran, Arabic grammar, and Islamic law. Recently Al-Azhar has added to its religious faculties a faculty of humanities and sciences, and has opened its doors to women students. Kairouine University, which is also passing through a similar transitional stage, has about a thousand women students out of an enrollment of some six thousand.

Three American universities have played a significant role in education in the Arab world: the American University of Beirut in Lebanon, established in 1866; the American University of Cairo, established in 1919; and the Beirut College for Women, established in 1924. The American University of Beirut is the largest, with 2,600 students, of fifty-two nationalities and twenty-four religions.

Students examine slides in a botany class at Faculty of Arts and Science, Baghdad University.

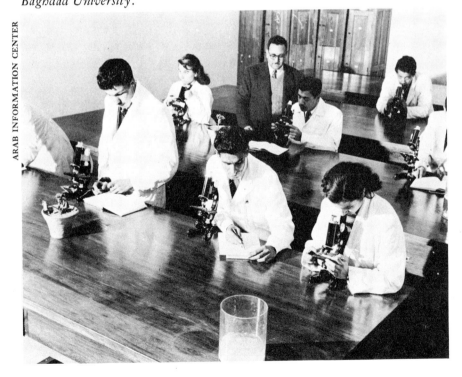

Bazaars and Bargaining

BAZAAR SHOPPING and bargaining are a way of life in Arab lands. The Arab people enjoy hunting for bargains in bazaars almost as much as do the tourists, who find Arab bazaars completely irresistible.

What is a bazaar like? It is a labyrinth of winding, narrow lanes with tiny, frontless shops, which are closed at night by pulling down corrugated iron shutters. Bazaars are sometimes roofed with matting or concrete vaulting to keep out the hot sun. This gives them an intriguing, mysterious light.

Crowds of shoppers throng the lanes of the bazaars; men in long robes and turbans; the coffee man carrying a huge copper coffeepot and clanking two brass saucers to announce his coming; basket boys waiting to carry home a customer's purchases; the bread boy walking unconcernedly with a tray of pancake-like Arabic bread on his head.

Articles are made, as well as sold, in bazaars. There are separate lanes for copper workers, jewelers, carpenters, shoemakers, and leatherworkers. And there is an endless variety of things to buy: exotic perfumes, camel saddles, gold bangles, silver anklets, aromatic herbs, giant leather hassocks, beak-spouted copper coffeepots, red, yellow, or blue leather sandals, oriental rugs, pots and pans, pistachio

THOMAS J. GARTLAND

The Baghdad bazaar is crowded with shoppers, and artisans who work at a variety of trades.

nuts, rose water, fruit, vegetables, and a dozen kinds of candy tantalizingly displayed in glass jars.

Bargaining is one of the great pleasures of bazaar shoppers, and of shopkeepers as well. They consider bargaining a battle of wits. In bargaining, the shopkeeper first names a price for his merchandise. It is always a higher price than he expects to get. The shopper immediately says the price is too high, and starts to point out the defects of the merchandise. The shopkeeper praises his product to the skies. Then the shopper offers a lower price than he expects to pay. The shopkeeper expresses amazement. Then a verbal battle of wits is on. At this point a crowd often gathers to enjoy the fun. Sometimes the shopper will start to walk away, as if he were finished with the whole transaction. If the shopkeeper is willing to make one more concession, he will run after the customer and they will settle on the final price. Bargaining is always friendly. Nobody ever gets angry, however the deal turns out.

Some of the most colorful and exotic bazaars of Arab cities are the Musky bazaar in Cairo, Egypt, the covered bazaars of Aleppo (Haleb), Syria, the Hamidiyyah bazaar of Damascus, Syria, the copper bazaar of Baghdad, Iraq, the arcaded bazaars of Tunis, Tunisia. At the Djemaa-el-Fna in Marrakesh, Morocco, you can not only shop, but you can also watch the performances of snake charmers, fire-eaters, acrobats, and *chleuh* dancers, and listen to storytellers.

THOMAS J. GARTLAND

A metalworker displays his wares in the Baghdad bazaar.

Holidays and Games

THE TWO most important festivals of the year in Arab lands — days when everyone stops work and when feasts and parties are held — are 'Id al-Fitr and 'Id al-Adha, both Muslim holidays. 'Id al-Fitr comes at the end of the fast of Ramadan, and is a three-day festival. 'Id al-Adha is a four-day festival which ends the pilgrimage to Mecca.

Children are given presents of new clothes for these holidays. They go with their parents to call on friends, bringing gifts of cookies and pastries. For the holiday feast a whole lamb is roasted with a stuffing of rice, almonds, and pine nuts. Part of the lamb is always given to the poor.

Children look forward to the holidays because they know that merry-go-rounds will be set up in parks, and that the man with the trained bear, or the man with the trained donkey, will be in town. The "galla-galla" man will be doing his tricks with copper cups under which a tiny yellow chicken appears and disappears miraculously. At night there will be storytelling under the stars, and perhaps dancing horses, performing to the flute, the drums, and the *al'ud* (a lutelike instrument).

ARAB INFORMATION CENTER

A volleyball game is played by students of the Sana'a High School in Yemen.

Pilgrims pray at the Stations of the Cross on the Via Dolorosa in Jerusalem, Jordan, on Good Friday

Easter is the most important Christian holiday in the Arab world. Thousands of pilgrims go to Jerusalem in Jordan during Easter week to pray at the Stations of the Cross on the Via Dolorosa, and to participate in services at the Church of the Holy Sepulchre which marks the site of the Crucifixion and Resurrection of Jesus.

Christian Arab children celebrate Easter more than Christmas. They help their mothers decorate Easter cookies, which are served to guests on Easter Sunday. One of the Easter games for children is egg cracking. On Easter morning, boys and girls are given bags of decorated hard-boiled eggs by their mothers. They knock eggs, end to end, with their playmates, and the child who cracks his friend's egg wins it. The goal of the game is to come home with as many eggs as possible in one's bag.

Favorite sports in Arab lands are tennis, basketball, water-skiing, soccer, volleyball, jumping, weight lifting, and swimming. There is skiing in the mountains of Morocco and Lebanon. Pan-Arab Olympic Games are held from time to time in the athletic stadiums of various Arab countries, with athletes competing for awards.

53

Food and Hospitality

"AHLAN WA SAHLAN" is an oft-repeated phrase in the Arab world. It means, "You are welcome." And visitors to Arab homes are genuinely and sincerely welcome, for according to a centuries-old tradition the guest is considered a sacred trust.

Whether you visit a Bedouin's tent in the desert, or the palatial villa of a city dweller, or a farmer's mud-brick home, you will be warmly greeted with many polite phrases of welcome and served the traditional coffee or tea which is a symbol of Arab hospitality. Even shopkeepers may offer you a tiny cup of Arabic coffee, a glass of mint tea, or lemonade.

When a guest enters an Arab home, everyone in the room rises. The guest moves around the circle, shaking hands with each person. Many welcoming phrases are exchanged, and inquiries are made about the guest's health and welfare. If a guest has some request to make or business to discuss, it is postponed until just before his departure. It is not polite to leave your host's house until you have taken a cup of coffee, or a cup of tea, or a glass of fruit juice, or at least a piece of candy.

Though food in Arab lands may vary from country to country, everyone likes and eats bread. Arabic bread is usually a round, pancake-like, flat loaf, the size of a dinner plate and sometimes hollow inside. But you will also find bread of a French type, and thicker loaves of the pancake type of bread. One of the unique and delicious breads of the Arab world is the round, paper-thin village bread found in some of the eastern Arab countries. It is almost a yard in diameter. It is cooked on a very hot, convex griddle, usually in an out-of-door oven, and is folded into a triangle when served.

Holiday feasts or feasts to celebrate some special occasion are lavish in the abundance of food served. A big feast in Morocco, Algeria, or Tunisia is called a *diffa*. It includes a long succession of mouth-watering dishes, including puff pastries stuffed with pigeon meat, roast lamb, salads, roast chicken, and *couscous*. Honey cakes or other sweet pastries, fruits, and mint tea complete the *diffa*.

Couscous is the main dish in Arab countries of North Africa as far east as Libya. It is made of semolina, a hard-wheat grain, steamed over a pot of vegetable soup. During the steaming process, the semolina is taken out and rolled once, or perhaps several times. Vegetables such as carrots, turnips, potatoes, onions, and greens, and pieces of lamb, beef, chicken, or sometimes fish are served with the *couscous*.

Eastward from Libya, rice becomes the staple dish, and lamb the popular meat. Rice is always served at the main noon meal, sometimes as a side course, sometimes mixed with ground lamb

An Iraqi farmer climbs a date palm to harvest the fruit.

A farm girl of the United Arab Republic.

and pine nuts and used as a stuffing for such vegetables as small green squash, tomatoes, grape leaves, or cabbage leaves. Fruit is greatly appreciated and widely eaten in Arab lands. Often one hears people praising the grapes or the apples of their native village, or the golden, honey-sweet dates of a particular oasis.

An Arab city famous for its sweets is Damascus, Syria. Glazed fruits are its specialty: tiny pears, plums, peaches, apples, or apricots, grown in Damascus fruit groves, and lightly coated with sugar syrup. They are packed in beautiful mosaic boxes, inlaid by Damascus artisans with tiny pieces of wood, mother-of-pearl, and ivory.

Chewy ice cream is another of the novel sweets made in Damascus. It acquires its "elastic" texture from a beating process. First the ice cream is turned, until it gets thick, in a brass pot which sets inside a barrel of ice and salt. Then the mixture is beaten with a wooden paddle. It is served by winding the ice cream skillfully into a glass dish. It is chewy when you eat it. There are many flavors: lemon, vanilla, chocolate, orange, and banana.

Arab lands are no place for persons who must watch their weight, particularly if they are guests and are being entertained royally, as all guests are.

Ma As-Salamah

ONE of the delightful aspects of Arab lands is their relaxed atmosphere. The pace of life is slower than in the Western world. People are not always hurrying in frantic haste to get somewhere or to get something done.

"Haste comes from the devil" is a famous Arab proverb.

Arab lands are moving ahead, but maintaining the deliberate pace best understood by their people and in keeping with their tempo of life.

There seems to be more time in Arab lands to enjoy the variety of experiences that make up a day.

There is always time to chat with a friend or an acquaintance on the street or in an office, and to enjoy a cup of coffee together.

There is always time to bargain in a bazaar, and to linger until the best bargain is arrived at.

There is always time to enjoy a sunset on the Mediterranean, sipping tea or coffee or lemonade in a garden café.

There is always time to receive guests graciously when they come to pay a visit — even unexpected guests.

There is always time to pray — five times a day.

There is always time to be polite — to shower upon friends and acquaintances the cordial, friendly compliments or words of solicitude with which the Arabic language is so richly endowed.

The days in Arab lands somehow seem long enough to include all these pleasant, gracious aspects of living, as well as the hard work and the tireless efforts of each country to build a new life for its people.

Even the farewell in Arab lands is like a benediction. It is *Ma as-salamah*, "May you go in peace."

What of the Future?

ARAB LANDS are facing many decades of hard work and self-discipline to bring a better life to their people. The crusade is against illiteracy, poverty, and disease. More schools are needed, more teachers, more textbooks. Better housing is needed, more nutritious food, clean water. Teams of medical and sanitation workers are needed to help eradicate such diseases as malaria, bilharziasis, and trachoma, which still bring death and blindness to thousands of the Arab people. Clinics are needed to teach baby and child care, nutrition, and personal hygiene to village mothers.

Progress is being made in all these directions. But it takes time and money to carry out such programs. It has been estimated, for example, that it will take Egypt forty years to equip its 14,000 villages with enough schools and medical clinics to meet pressing needs. So many things are needed so quickly in Arab lands that it takes great fortitude and balance for Arab governments and socially conscious Arab people to face the future without being discouraged.

To secure a national income sufficient to finance urgently needed programs, each country must export more than it imports; provide jobs with sufficient income to enable its citizens to pay income taxes for the support of their government; industrialize in order to add to the value of natural resources; or seek assistance from foreign governments.

How can goals be achieved with limited budgets? What projects should have priority? How can the farmers be aroused to their role in a democracy after years of servitude, spent in working as tenant farmers for landlords of large estates? These are just a few of the questions which challenge the Arab countries, particularly those countries which attained their freedom less than a decade ago and

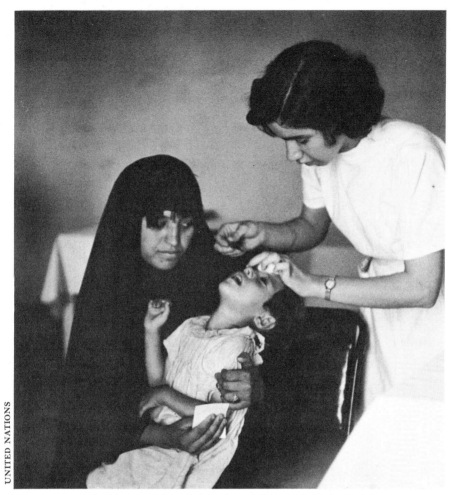

A village mother brings her child to a health clinic.

do not have oil money to finance their programs.

Industrialization requires capital, hydroelectric power, natural resources, and skilled workers and technicians. Technical schools are being opened in most Arab countries to train much-needed mechanics, machine operators, electricians, and construction workers. The Arab people are highly intelligent and quick to learn. Even Bedouins of the desert have come, within a quarter of a century, to

Modern schools are being built as fast as possible in Arab lands.

At a training center in Tripoli, Libya, an instructor describes to students the parts of a car engine. This training center for technical and clerical help was set up in 1951 with the help of the International Labor Organization and UNESCO.

hold responsible administrative and technical positions with the oil companies. But industrialization cannot take place overnight.

In lands of limited or no rainfall, modernization of agriculture, irrigation, better use of available water supplies, and reclamation of land are long-term projects in the endless fight against the ever-encroaching deserts.

There has been talk of Arab unity, of all Arab lands combining in a federation to pool resources and cooperate in the solution of mutual problems. Such a federation does not appear to be immediately on the horizon. Meanwhile the League of Arab States (popularly known as the Arab League) is one unifying force, offering a forum or a small "United Nations" of Arab lands, where problems can be discussed and policies coordinated.

The Arab lands are strategically important lands — gateway countries to Africa, to Asia, and to the Orient. For this reason their political stability, their economic progress, and the speed with which they can provide a better life for their people are of supreme and urgent importance to the entire world.

This Bedouin of the desert has learned to work with technical instruments.

Governments of Arab Lands

Country	Form of Government	Independence Achieved*
Algeria	Republic	July 3, 1962
Egypt (United Arab Republic)	Republic	June 18, 1953
Iraq	Republic	June 14, 1958
Jordan	Constitutional monarchy	May 25, 1946
Kuwait	Sheikhdom	June 19, 1961
Lebanon	Republic	November 22, 1946
Libya	Federated monarchy	December 24, 1951
Morocco	Constitutional monarchy	December 7, 1962
Saudi Arabia	Hereditary monarchy	Established 1932
Sudan	Republic	January 1, 1956
Syria	Republic	April 17, 1946
Tunisia	Republic	March 20, 1956
Yemen	Republic	September 26, 1962

In addition, there are the following sheikhdoms, sultanates, etc.:

Country	Form of Government	Independence Achieved*
Bahrain	Sheikhdom	Independent (under British protection)
Qatar	Sheikhdom	Independent (under British protection)
Trucial States	Sheikhdoms	Independent (under British protection)
Muscat and Oman	Sultanates	Independent
Aden Protectorate	Sheikhdoms	Under British protection
Aden	British	(British-occupied in 1839)

*Fully free of occupation by conquerors, mandatory powers, special treaty concessions, etc.

Index

Abbasid Caliphate, 32, 34
Abraham, 26
Abu-Bakr, 22
Aden, 62
Aden Protectorate, 4, 44, 62
Ahmed ibn Tulun Mosque, 1, 38
Al-Azhar University, 48-49
Aleppo, 35, 51
Alexandria, 30, 43
Al-Farabi, 1
Algeria, 30, 34, 39, 44, 55, 62
Alhambra, 1, 38
Al-Idrisi, 1
Al-Kindi, 1
Allah, 21
"Arab bridge," 36-37
Arab countries, 4, 6, 62
Arab Empire, 1, 32-35
Arab lands: Americans in, 44, 49; diseases in, 58; future of, 58; occupation of, by European powers, 39; tempo of life in, 57
Arab League, 39, 61
Arab unity, 61
Arabian Peninsula, 16, 28
Arabic language, 1, 17, 20, 32, 34; as decoration, 18; English words derived from, 18, 20
Arabs, 1, 4, 32; arts of, 1, 37, 50; as a people, 1, 4; courtesy of, 15; daily life of, 7-16; dress of, 8, 11-13; dwellings of, 8, 14, 16; education of, 39, 47-49; family ties of, 15-16; food of, 13, 16, 34, 54-56; history of, 28-38; holidays of, 52-53; hospitality of, 54; language of, 1, 17, 18, 20, 32, 34; legacy of, to West, 36-38; occupations of, 8, 9, 13, 41-45; recreations

of, 10, 14, 17, 50-56; religion of, 1, 21-27, 34; sports of, 53; village, 11-14
Architecture, Arab, 38
Arts, Arab, 1, 37
Aswan, 43
Averroës, 1
Avicenna, 1
Ayyubid Dynasty, 34

Baalbek Summer Festival, 10
Baghdad, 35, 51
Bahrain, 4, 44, 62
Bargaining, 50-51
Bazaars, 50-51
Bedouins, 16, 59
Books, Arab, 20
Boxes, mosaic (Damascus), 56
Berbers, 30
Bread, Arab, 54

Cairo, 1, 48, 49, 51
Caliph Othman, 22
Caliphs, 32
Christianity, 1, 34
Christians, Arab, 27, 53
Citadel (Aleppo), 38
Citadel (Cairo), 1
Climate, 6
Cordova, 30
Cordova, University of, 36
Courtesy, Arab, 15
Couscous, 55
Crusades, 34-35

Damascus, 1, 30, 32, 34, 35, 51, 56
Deserts, 6; Arabian, 6; Sahara, 6
Diffa, 55
Diseases, 58

63

Persia, 30
Poetry contests, 17
Proper names, Arab, 20

Qatar, 4, 44, 62

Rainfall, 6
Ramadan, 24
Recreations, Arab, 10, 14, 17, 50-56
Religion, Arab, 1, 21-27, 34
Rhazes, 1
Richard the Lionhearted, 34
Roderick the Visigoth, 30
Root words, Arabic, 17

Saladin, 34
Saudi Arabia, 4, 44, 45, 62
Seville, 30
Spain, 1, 30, 35, 38
Sports, in Arab lands, 53
"Standing before God," 26
"Stoning," 26
Storytelling, 20, 52
Street vendors, 7
Sudan, 4, 6, 41, 62
Sultan Hassan Mosque, 1

Syria, 4, 6, 30, 35, 38, 39, 41, 43, 51, 56, 62

Tartars, 35
Technical schools, 59-61
Tigris River, 6, 28, 41
Toledo, 30
Tourism, 45
Trucial States, 4, 44, 62
Tunisia, 30, 38, 39, 41, 44, 51, 55, 62

Umayyad Caliphate, 32, 34
Umayyad Mosque, 1, 34
United Arab Republic, *see* Egypt
United Nations, 39, 40
Universities, 48; American, in Arab lands, 49

Veil, wearing of, 12-13
Village living, 11-14

Women, position of, 8-9, 13

Yarmuk River, 41
Yemen, 4, 41, 62

Zionists, 39-40

FIRST BOOKS
classified by subject
Some titles are listed in more than one category

The ARTS

Architecture	Gardening	Poetry
Ballet	How to Fix It	Puppets
Bells	Jazz	Rhythms
Color	Music	Stage Costume and
Drawing	Paintings	Make-Up
	Photography	

COMMUNICATIONS

Atlas	Letter Writing	Public Libraries
Codes and Ciphers	Maps and Globes	Teaching Machines
Language & How To	Measurement	Television
Use It	Printing	Words

SCIENCE

Air	Electricity	Roads
Airplanes	Food	Science Experiments
Antarctic	Glaciers	Sea Shells
Archaeology	Glass	Snakes
Architecture	Human Senses	Sound
Astronomy	Light	Space Travel
Automobiles	Machines	Stone Age Man
Bees	Mammals	Stones
Bells	Maps and Globes	Submarines
Birds	Measurement	Television
Bridges	Microbes	Tools
Bugs	Mining	Trains
Caves	Ocean	Trees
Color	Photography	Tropical Mammals
Conservation	Plants	Water
Cotton	Prehistoric Animals	Weather
Earth	Rhythms	Wild Flowers

SPORTS & HOBBIES

Baseball	Dogs	Photography
Basketball	Dolls	Physical Fitness
Boys' Cooking	Football	Sailing
Cartoons for Kids	Gardening	Stones
Cats	Horses	Surprising Facts
Chess	How to Fix It	Swimming
Christmas Joy	Jokes	
Codes and Ciphers	Magic	

SOCIAL STUDIES
United States

Atlas	Hawaii	Oregon Trail
American History	Holidays	Panama Canal
American Revolution	Indian Wars	Pioneers
California Gold Rush	Indians	Presidents
The China Clippers	National Monuments	Supreme Court
Civil War Land Battles	National Parks	United Nations
Civil War Naval Actions	Negroes	War of 1812
Congress	New England	Washington, D.
Constitution	New World Explorers	World War I
Early Settlers		World War II

The World About Us

Africa	Communist China	Mexico
Ancient Bible Lands	Congo	Netherlands
Ancient Egypt	England	New Zealand
Ancient Mesopotamia	Eskimos	Ocean
and Persia	Festivals	Pakistan
Ancient Greece	France	South America
Ancient Rome	Ghana	Soviet Union
Antarctic	India	United Nations
Archaeology	Israel	Vikings
Australia	Italy	West Germany
Barbarian Invaders	Japan	West Indies
Brazil	Kings	World War I
Canada	Medieval Man	World War II
	Mediterranean	

People and Products

Conservation	Firemen	Nurses
Cotton	Food	Supermarkets
Cowboys	Glass	Water

LITERATURE & LANGUAGE ARTS

Codes and Ciphers	Letter Writing	Norse Legends
Color	Legendary Beings	Poetry
Fairy Tales	Maps and Globes	Printing
Language & How To	Mythology	Teaching Mach
Use It	Mythical Beasts	Words

TRANSPORTATION

Airplanes	Maps and Globes	Space Travel
Automobiles	Panama Canal	Trains
Boats	Roads	Water
Bridges	Ships	